# WHAT ARE MADE OF?

by Debbie Vilardi

**Cody Koala**
An Imprint of Pop!
popbooksonline.com

**abdobooks.com**

Published by Pop!, a division of ABDO, PO Box 398166, Minneapolis, Minnesota 55439. Copyright © 2019 by POP, LLC. International copyrights reserved in all countries. No part of this book may be reproduced in any form without written permission from the publisher. Pop!™ is a trademark and logo of POP, LLC.

Printed in the United States of America, North Mankato, Minnesota

082018
012019

THIS BOOK CONTAINS RECYCLED MATERIALS

Cover Photo: iStockphoto
Interior Photos: iStockphoto, 1, 6, 18; Shutterstock Images, 5 (top), 5 (bottom left), 5 (bottom right), 9, 10–11, 13, 14, 16–17, 21

Editor: Meg Gaertner
Series Designer: Laura Mitchell

**Library of Congress Control Number: 2018949243**

**Publisher's Cataloging-in-Publication Data**

Names: Vilardi, Debbie, author.
Title: What are clouds made of? / by Debbie Vilardi.
Description: Minneapolis, Minnesota : Pop!, 2019 | Series: Science questions | Includes online resources and index.
Identifiers: ISBN 9781532162145 (lib. bdg.) | ISBN 9781641855853 (pbk) | ISBN 9781532163203 (ebook)
Subjects: LCSH: Clouds--Juvenile literature. | Clouds--Thermodynamics--Juvenile literature. | Weather--Juvenile literature. | Children's questions and answers--Juvenile literature.
Classification: DDC 500--dc23

## Hello! My name is

# Cody Koala

Pop open this book and you'll find QR codes like this one, loaded with information, so you can learn even more!

Scan this code* and others like it while you read, or visit the website below to make this book pop.

**popbooksonline.com/clouds-made-of**

*Scanning QR codes requires a web-enabled smart device with a QR code reader app and a camera.

# Table of Contents

# Clouds

White, fluffy clouds mean fair weather. Large gray clouds can bring rain or snow. Clouds come in many colors and shapes. But all clouds form the same way.

**Watch a video here!**

# Water Vapor

Clouds form out of **water vapor**. The sun heats the water in lakes and oceans. The water **evaporates** and becomes a gas.

Complete an activity here!

The water vapor rises in the sky. It cools down. It connects with dust, dirt, and other tiny **particles**.

The particles can include smoke, sea salt, ash, and **pollutants**.

# Chapter 3

# Condensation

The water vapor **condenses** around these particles. Small drops form. They freeze if the air is cold enough.

Learn more here!

Many drops of
water or ice join together.
A cloud forms.

Clouds can be very heavy.

But they do not fall.

Some clouds weigh
as much as
100 elephants.

The cloud's weight is spread out over many drops. The drops are not heavy enough to fall. The wind pushes up against them.

Clouds are mostly air and water.

# Chapter 4

# Stormy Weather

Sometimes the drops in a cloud join together. They combine into heavier drops. The cloud grows dark. Sunlight cannot pass through.

Learn more here!

The cloud carries a lot of water. The water drops fall when they are heavy enough.

They can fall as rain. If it is cold enough, they can fall as ice or snow.

Clouds form as part of the water cycle. This is the process of water changing from one form to another.

# Water Cycle

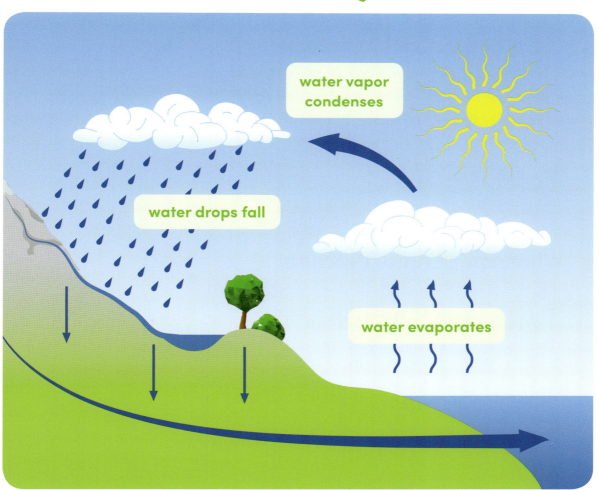

water vapor condenses

water drops fall

water evaporates

# Making Connections

## Text-to-Self

Fog is a low-floating cloud. Have you ever walked through fog? What was it like?

## Text-to-Text

Have you read other books about the weather? What new thing did you learn?

## Text-to-World

Imagine a world without clouds. How would the world be different?

# Glossary

**condense** – change from a gas to a liquid.

**evaporate** – change from a liquid to a gas.

**particle** – a tiny piece of something.

**pollutant** – something that makes the water or air dirty.

**water vapor** – water in the form of a gas.

# Index

## Online Resources

# popbooksonline.com

Thanks for reading this Cody Koala book!

Scan this code* and others like it in this book, or visit the website below to make this book pop!

**popbooksonline.com/clouds-made-of**

*Scanning QR codes requires a web-enabled smart device with a QR code reader app and a camera.